Ultimate

KRAFT ®
PHILADELPHIA ®
BRAND
CREAM CHEESE
PASTEURIZED

CHEESECAKES

Publications International, Ltd.

Photographs on pages 17, 21, 31, 35, 39, 45, 55 and 67, copyright © Publications International, Ltd.

This edition published by Publications International, Ltd., 7373 N. Cicero Ave., Lincolnwood, IL 60646.

Marketing: Robert Beuther
Director, Kraft Creative Kitchens: Marilyn Kruse
Brand Kitchens Manager, Kraft Creative Kitchens: Maureen Weiss
Design & Art Direction: Roberta Kozuch & Associates
Coordinator: Tracy Patun
Recipe Development: Marla Goldberg, Bev Dillon, Marie Jirsa, Sara Kline
Food Stylists: Amy Andrews, Patricia Godsted, Bonnie Rabert, Teri Rys-Maki
Food Stylists' Assistants: Karyn Wexler, Laura Hess, Carol Pearson
Photographers: Joe Polivka; John Polich; Sacco Productions Limited, Chicago
Prop Stylists: Cindy Neberz, Kathy Lapin
Editors: Betty Heinlen, Molly Hamilton
Administrative Assistant: Joan Baur
Consumer Promotions: Jeff Tolke, Marsha Link

Pictured on the front cover: PHILLY 3-STEP™ Caramel Apple Cheesecake *(page 48)*.

Pictured on the back cover *(clockwise from top left):* PHILLY 3-STEP™ Coconut Cheesecake *(page 66)*, Heavenly Cheesecake *(page 44)* and PHILLY 3-STEP™ Midwest Cheesecake *(page 54)*.

ISBN: 0-7853-1765-1

Manufactured in U.S.A.

8 7 6 5 4 3 2 1

Prep time includes the amount of time it takes to get ready to prepare the recipe. Whenever possible, steps are combined to save time.

Cooking time includes the time it takes to cook the ingredients (i.e., to bake, simmer, brown, etc.).

CHEESECAKES

PREPARATION TIPS

CHEESECAKE RECIPES

*W*HO SAYS DELICIOUS CHEESECAKES CAN'T BE SIMPLE? Now anyone can make cheesecake with the new *PHILLY 3-STEP™ Cheesecake.* A cheesecake that has three simple steps—mix, pour, bake—and takes only 10 minutes to prepare and 40 minutes to bake! It's *easy* to make but still tastes rich, creamy and delicious. Simply mix together the 4 ingredients, pour into a graham cracker crust and bake. That's it! The Kraft Creative Kitchens have developed over 26 sensational flavor variations of the recipe, including *Pumpkin* and *White Chocolate Almond.*

For you cheesecake connoisseurs who want to make a cheesecake in a springform pan, we're presenting some of our most popular showstopping recipes. Tall and elegant cheesecakes, from the truly classic *New York Cheesecake* to the innovative *Brownie Bottom Cheesecake.*

Have you ever met a cheesecake you didn't like? Of course, to make the finest possible cheesecake, you must select the ultimate in high quality cream cheese. PHILADELPHIA BRAND Cream Cheese is the choice for a perfect cheesecake every time. And for a luscious lower fat cheesecake, try substituting PHILADELPHIA BRAND Neufchatel Cheese, 1/3 Less Fat than Cream Cheese or PHILADELPHIA BRAND FREE Fat Free Cream Cheese for cream cheese! Ready to begin? You bet. Piece of cake. Enjoy!

Philly 3-Step™ Cheesecake

Prep time: *10 min.* Cooking time: *40 min.*

2 (8 oz.) pkgs. PHILADELPHIA BRAND Cream Cheese, softened
½ cup sugar
½ teaspoon vanilla
2 eggs
1 KEEBLER READY CRUST™ Graham Cracker Pie Crust (6 oz. *or* 9 inch)

1. MIX cream cheese, sugar and vanilla at medium speed with electric mixer until well blended. Add eggs; mix until blended.

2. POUR into crust.

3. BAKE at 350° F, 40 minutes or until center is almost set. Cool. Refrigerate 3 hours or overnight.

8 servings

Springform Pan Cheesecakes

Easy Steps Toward Success

For baked springform pan cheesecakes, prepare crust by pressing crust ingredients into pan. A mixture of graham cracker crumbs, sugar and melted PARKAY Spread Sticks is shown here.

Beat PHILADELPHIA BRAND Cream Cheese and sugar at medium speed with electric mixer. Add eggs, one at a time, mixing at low speed after each addition, just until blended. For flavored cheesecakes, blend in flavorings, such as melted chocolate shown here.

Using a spatula, pour cheesecake batter into prepared pan. Bake for minimum time given in recipe or until center is almost set. Cool on wire rack.

Immediately upon removal from oven, run a thin metal spatula or knife around edge of cheesecake (pushing against side of pan) to loosen it from side of pan. Keep spring fastener on side of pan locked and springform pan side on. Cool 1 hour at room temperature; refrigerate.

Loosen spring fastener. Lift rim of pan straight up to separate it from cheesecake.

Place cheesecake on serving plate. Garnish as desired.

Tips from the Kraft Creative Kitchens

To prevent cracking follow these quick mixing and baking hints:

MIXING

- *Soften PHILLY Cream Cheese before mixing.* To soften in microwave: place one unwrapped (8 oz.) package in microwavable bowl. Microwave on HIGH 15 seconds. Add 15 seconds for each additional package of PHILLY Cream Cheese.
- *Don't overbeat.* Beat at low speed after adding eggs, just until blended.
- *Gently stir in* any flavoring ingredients (chocolate chips, fruit, etc.) at the very end of mixing.

BAKING

- *Bake in a moist oven.* When preheating oven, place 13 x 9-inch baking pan half filled with hot tap water on bottom rack of oven. Bake cheesecake on middle rack above pan of water.
- *Don't peek* into oven during baking.
- *Don't overbake.* When done, edges should be slightly puffed. The center area, about the size of a silver dollar, should still appear soft and moist. The center will firm upon cooling.

COOLING

- Cool cheesecake on wire rack at room temperature for 1 hour before refrigerating.
- Refrigerate uncovered 3 to 4 hours or until thoroughly chilled. Place sheet of plastic wrap or foil across top of cheesecake; secure. Refrigerate overnight or up to 2 days.
- For best results, top or garnish cheesecake within 1 to 3 hours of serving, depending on stability of selected topping.
- To enhance flavor, remove cheesecake from refrigerator 30 minutes before serving.

FREEZING

- Prepare cheesecake as directed, omitting topping. Wrap securely in plastic wrap; overwrap with foil. Place in plastic bag; label, date and seal. Freeze up to 2 months.
- Thaw wrapped cheesecake in refrigerator overnight.
- Individual slices should be cut and wrapped before freezing. Thaw 1 slice in microwave on DEFROST (30% power) for 45 to 60 seconds. Let stand about 5 minutes before serving.

LEAN & LUSCIOUS

- Substitute PHILLY Neufchatel Cheese, 1/3 Less Fat Than Cream Cheese *or* PHILLY FREE Fat Free Cream Cheese for cream cheese in any of these recipes.

Creative Crusts

Whether you are making a classic cheesecake in a springform pan or a PHILLY 3-STEP™ Cheesecake, these creative crusts are sure to be a hit.

Graham Cracker Crust:
Mix 1½ cups graham cracker crumbs, 3 tablespoons sugar and ⅓ cup PARKAY Spread Sticks, melted. Press onto bottom and sides of 9-inch pie plate or bottom of springform pan. Pour cheesecake batter into unbaked crust.

Spiced Graham Cracker Crust:
Add ½ teaspoon ground cinnamon or ¼ teaspoon ground ginger.

Nut Crust:
Substitute ½ cup finely chopped pecans, almonds, walnuts, peanuts or macadamia nuts for ½ cup of the graham cracker crumbs.

Vanilla Wafer Crust:
Substitute 1½ cups vanilla wafer crumbs for graham cracker crumbs.

Chocolate Cookie Crust:
Omit sugar and reduce PARKAY Spread Sticks to 2 tablespoons. Substitute finely crushed chocolate sandwich cookies for graham cracker crumbs.

Sumptuous Sauces

Serve your cheesecake with one of these deliciously easy sauces.

Chocolate Orange Sauce:
Mix 1 cup chocolate ice cream topping and 1 tablespoon orange-flavored liqueur. Makes 8 to 12 servings.

Southern Caramel Sauce:
Mix 1 cup caramel ice cream topping and 2 teaspoons bourbon or brandy. Makes 8 to 12 servings.

Strawberry Sauce:
Place 1 pkg. (10 oz.) frozen strawberries, thawed, in food processor or blender container fitted with steel blade; cover. Process until smooth. Strain. Stir in 1 to 2 tablespoons orange-flavored liqueur or orange juice. Makes 8 to 12 servings.

Crimson Raspberry Sauce:
Place 2 pkgs. (10 oz. each) frozen raspberries, thawed, in heavy 2-quart saucepan. Bring to a boil. Boil over high heat, stirring frequently, 7 minutes. Strain. Stir in 1 teaspoon fresh lemon juice. For *Creamy Raspberry Sauce*, stir in 3 tablespoons whipping cream. Makes 8 to 12 servings.

Great Garnishes

Try these finishing touches to make your cheesecakes extra special.

Shaving Chocolate

Pull vegetable peeler across surface of 1 square BAKER'S Semi-Sweet Chocolate; sprinkle over cheesecake.

Citrus Fruit Twists

Cut 1 lemon, lime or orange into slices. Discard slices toward ends. Make small cut in middle of each slice from center down through peel. Twist slices into spirals.

Toasting Nuts

Spread nuts in shallow pan. Bake at 400°F, stirring frequently, 8 to 10 minutes or until golden brown.

Piped Borders

Insert star tip into pastry bag; fill with COOL WHIP Whipped Topping or whipped cream. Squeeze onto cheesecake to make desired border.

Chocolate Leaves

- Melt 4 squares BAKER'S Semi-Sweet Chocolate. Using narrow spatula or brush, spread chocolate over undersides of washed and dried non-toxic leaves (such as lemon, rose or grape ivy) to form smooth, thick coating. Avoid spreading chocolate to very edge of leaf to prevent chocolate from running onto top side of leaf. Place leaves on wax paper-lined tray. Refrigerate 15 minutes or until chocolate is firm.
- Carefully peel away leaves from chocolate. Refrigerate chocolate leaves until ready to use.

Toasting Coconut

Spread BAKER'S ANGEL FLAKE Coconut in shallow pan. Bake at 350°F, stirring frequently, 7 to 12 minutes or until lightly browned.

Dipping Fruit and Nuts

Melt BAKER'S Semi-Sweet Chocolate. Dip fruit or nuts into melted chocolate, covering at least half; let excess chocolate drip off. Arrange on wax paper-lined tray. Refrigerate until chocolate is firm. *Do not freeze.*

Quick Toppers

■ Drizzle caramel or chocolate ice cream topping over cheesecake just before serving.

■ Spread sour cream or COOL WHIP Whipped Topping over cheesecake; top with fresh fruit slices.

■ Spoon canned pie filling over cheesecake.

■ For a beautiful design, place paper doily or cut paper pattern on top of cheesecake. Sprinkle generously with powdered sugar or unsweetened cocoa. Carefully lift doily with a straight upward motion.

Chocolate Drizzle

■ Place 1 square BAKER'S Semi-Sweet Chocolate in plastic zippered sandwich bag. Close bag tightly. Microwave on HIGH about 1 minute or until chocolate is melted. Fold down top of bag tightly; snip tiny piece off 1 corner.

■ Holding top of bag tightly, drizzle chocolate through opening over plain or fruit topped cheesecake.

Chocolate Doodles

Melt chocolate, following directions for Chocolate Drizzle. Drizzle chocolate into free-form designs onto wax paper-lined cookie sheet. Or, draw design on paper, cover with wax paper and drizzle chocolate over design. Refrigerate until firm, about 30 minutes.

Philly 3-Step™ Chocolate Chip Cheesecake

An all-time favorite.

Prep time: *10 min.* **Cooking time:** *40 min.*

2   (8 oz.) pkgs. PHILADELPHIA BRAND Cream Cheese, softened

½   cup sugar

½   teaspoon vanilla

2   eggs

¾   cup mini semi-sweet chocolate chips, divided

1   KEEBLER READY CRUST™ Graham Cracker *or* Chocolate Flavored Pie Crust (6 oz. *or* 9 inch)

1. MIX cream cheese, sugar and vanilla at medium speed with electric mixer until well blended. Add eggs; mix until blended. Stir in ½ cup of the chips.

2. POUR into crust. Sprinkle with remaining ¼ cup chips.

3. BAKE at 350°F, 40 minutes or until center is almost set. Cool. Refrigerate 3 hours or overnight.   *8 servings*

Peanut Butter Chocolate Chip: Beat ⅓ cup peanut butter in with cream cheese.

Banana Chocolate Chip: Beat ½ cup mashed ripe banana in with cream cheese.

Philly 3-Step™ Chocolate Lover's Cheesecake

Whip up this wonderful chocolate cheesecake in minutes!

Prep time: *10 min.* Cooking time: *40 min.*

2   (8 oz.) pkgs. PHILADELPHIA BRAND Cream Cheese, softened
½   cup sugar
½   teaspoon vanilla
2   eggs
4   squares BAKER'S Semi-Sweet Chocolate, melted, slightly cooled
1   KEEBLER READY CRUST™ Chocolate Flavored Pie Crust (6 oz. *or* 9 inch)

1. MIX cream cheese, sugar and vanilla at medium speed with electric mixer until well blended. Add eggs; mix until blended. Blend in melted chocolate.

2. POUR into crust.

3. BAKE at 350°F, 40 minutes or until center is almost set. Cool. Refrigerate 3 hours or overnight. Top with assorted fresh fruit, if desired.   *8 servings*

Mocha: Blend 3 tablespoons coffee-flavored liqueur or black coffee into batter.

Philly 3-Step™
White Chocolate Almond Cheesecake

Perfect for Hannukah or Christmas celebrations.

Prep time: *10 min.* Cooking time: *40 min.*

2	(8 oz.) pkgs. PHILADELPHIA BRAND Cream Cheese, softened
½	cup sugar
½	teaspoon vanilla
2	eggs
1	cup chopped white chocolate, divided
1	KEEBLER READY CRUST™ Graham Cracker Pie Crust (6 oz. *or* 9 inch)
½	cup chopped almonds

1. MIX cream cheese, sugar and vanilla at medium speed with electric mixer until well blended. Add eggs; mix until blended. Stir in ½ cup of the white chocolate.

2. POUR into crust. Sprinkle with almonds and remaining ½ cup white chocolate.

3. BAKE at 350°F, 40 minutes or until center is almost set. Cool. Refrigerate 3 hours or overnight.   *8 servings*

Chocolate Raspberry Cheesecake

A chocolate raspberry cheesecake covered with a decadent chocolate coating.

Prep time: *30 min.* Cooking time: *1 hour 20 min.*

CRUST

1½ cups finely crushed chocolate sandwich cookies
2   tablespoons PARKAY Spread Sticks, melted

FILLING

4   (8 oz.) pkgs. PHILADELPHIA BRAND Cream Cheese, softened, divided
¾   cup sugar
1   teaspoon vanilla
3   eggs
½   cup sour cream
6   squares BAKER'S Semi-Sweet Chocolate, melted, slightly cooled
⅓   cup strained red raspberry preserves

TOPPING

6   squares BAKER'S Semi-Sweet Chocolate
¼   cup whipping cream

- Heat oven to 325°F.

CRUST

- Mix crumbs and PARKAY spread; press onto bottom of 9-inch springform pan.

FILLING

- Beat 3 packages of the cream cheese, sugar and vanilla at medium speed with electric mixer until well blended. Add eggs, 1 at a time, mixing at low speed after each addition, just until blended. Blend in sour cream; pour over crust.
- Beat remaining cream cheese and 6 squares melted chocolate at medium speed on electric mixer until well blended. Add preserves; mix well. Drop rounded tablespoonfuls of chocolate mixture over plain cream cheese mixture; do not swirl.
- Bake 1 hour and 15 minutes to 1 hour and 20 minutes or until center is almost set. Run knife or metal spatula around rim of pan to loosen cake; cool before removing rim of pan.

TOPPING

- Melt remaining chocolate and whipping cream over low heat, stirring until smooth. Spread over cooled cheesecake. Refrigerate 4 hours or overnight. Garnish with COOL WHIP Whipped Topping, raspberries and mint leaves.   *12 servings*

Brownie Bottom Cheesecake

The best of both worlds! A fudgy brownie bottom topped with a creamy cheesecake.

Prep time: *40 min.* Cooking time: *1 hour*

BROWNIE BOTTOM
½ cup (1 stick) butter
4 squares BAKER'S Unsweetened Chocolate
1½ cups sugar
2 eggs
¼ cup milk
1 teaspoon vanilla
1 cup flour
½ teaspoon salt

CHEESECAKE
3 (8 oz.) pkgs. PHILADELPHIA BRAND Cream Cheese, softened
¾ cup sugar
1 teaspoon vanilla
3 eggs
½ cup sour cream

■ Heat oven to 325°F.

BROWNIE BOTTOM
■ Melt butter and chocolate in 3-quart heavy saucepan over low heat, stirring constantly; cool.
■ Add sugar and eggs, 1 at a time, mix until blended after each addition. Blend in milk and vanilla.
■ Stir in combined flour and salt, mixing just until blended.
■ Spoon into greased and floured 9x3-inch springform pan, spreading evenly.
■ Bake 25 minutes.

CHEESECAKE
■ Beat cream cheese, sugar and vanilla at medium speed with electric mixer until well blended. Add eggs, 1 at a time, mixing at low speed after each addition, just until blended.
■ Blend in sour cream; pour over brownie bottom (filling will almost come to top of pan).
■ Bake 55 to 60 minutes or until center is almost set. Run knife or metal spatula around rim of pan to loosen cake; cool before removing rim of pan. Refrigerate 4 hours or overnight. Let stand 30 minutes at room temperature before serving. Drizzle with assorted ice cream toppings, if desired.   *12 servings*

Chocolate Truffle Cheesecake

A sumptuous silky chocolate cheesecake.

Prep time: *30 min.* Cooking time: *1 hour 5 min.*

CRUST
1½ cups finely crushed chocolate sandwich cookies
2   tablespoons PARKAY Spread Sticks, melted

FILLING
3   (8 oz.) pkgs. PHILADELPHIA BRAND Cream Cheese,
     softened
1   cup sugar
1   teaspoon vanilla
3   eggs
8   squares BAKER'S Semi-Sweet Chocolate, melted,
     slightly cooled
¼   cup hazelnut liqueur (optional)

■   Heat oven to 325°F.

CRUST
■   Mix crumbs and PARKAY spread; press onto bottom of
     9-inch springform pan. Bake 10 minutes.

FILLING
■   Beat cream cheese, sugar and vanilla at medium speed with
     electric mixer until well blended. Add eggs, 1 at a time,
     mixing at low speed after each addition, just until blended.
     Blend in melted chocolate and liqueur; pour over crust.
■   Bake 60 to 65 minutes or until center is almost set.
     Run knife or metal spatula around rim of pan to loosen
     cake; cool before removing rim of pan. Refrigerate
     4 hours or overnight. Serve with Creamy Raspberry
     Sauce (p. 7), if desired.   *12 servings*

German Chocolate Cheesecake: Omit liqueur. Substitute
2 (4 oz.) pkgs. BAKER'S German Sweet Chocolate for the semi-sweet
chocolate. Bake and refrigerate as directed above. Cook ⅓ cup
evaporated milk, ⅓ cup sugar, ¼ cup (½ stick) PARKAY
Spread Sticks, 1 beaten egg and ½ teaspoon vanilla in small heavy
saucepan over low heat, stirring constantly, until thickened.
Stir in ½ cup BAKER'S ANGEL FLAKE Coconut and ½ cup
chopped pecans. Cool. Spread over cooled cheesecake.

Orange Chocolate Swirl Cheesecake

An exquisite blend of chocolate and orange.

Prep time: *30 min.* Cooking time: *1 hour*

CRUST

1½	cups graham cracker crumbs
¼	cup sugar
⅓	cup PARKAY Spread Sticks, melted

FILLING

3	(8 oz.) pkgs. PHILADELPHIA BRAND Cream Cheese, softened
1	cup sugar
5	.eggs
2	tablespoons orange-flavored liqueur *or* orange juice
½	teaspoon grated orange peel
4	squares BAKER'S Semi-Sweet Chocolate, melted, slightly cooled

■ Heat oven to 325°F.

CRUST

■ Mix crumbs, sugar and PARKAY spread; press onto bottom and 1½ - inches up sides of 9-inch springform pan. Bake 10 minutes.

FILLING

■ Beat cream cheese and sugar at medium speed with electric mixer until well blended. Add eggs, 1 at a time, mixing at low speed after each addition, just until blended. Blend in liqueur and peel.

■ Reserve 2 cups of the batter. Pour remaining cream cheese batter over crust. Blend chocolate into reserved batter. Add spoonfuls of the chocolate batter to the cream cheese batter. Cut through batters with knife several times for marble effect.

■ Bake 55 to 60 minutes or until center is almost set. Run knife or metal spatula around rim of pan to loosen cake; cool before removing rim of pan. Refrigerate 4 hours or overnight.

12 servings

White Chocolate Cheesecake

A crisp buttery cookie crust under a satiny white chocolate cheesecake.

Prep time: *35 min.* Cooking time: *1 hour*

CRUST

½   cup (1 stick) butter
¼   cup sugar
½   teaspoon vanilla
1   cup flour

FILLING

4   (8 oz.) pkgs. PHILADELPHIA BRAND Cream
    Cheese, softened
½   cup sugar
1   teaspoon vanilla
4   eggs
12 ozs. white chocolate, melted, slightly cooled

■ Heat oven to 325°F.

CRUST

■ Cream butter, sugar and vanilla in small bowl at medium speed with electric mixer until light and fluffy. Gradually add flour, mixing at low speed until blended. Press onto bottom of 9-inch springform pan; prick with fork.
■ Bake 25 minutes or until edges are light golden brown.

FILLING

■ Beat cream cheese, sugar and vanilla at medium speed with electric mixer until well blended. Add eggs, 1 at a time, mixing at low speed after each addition, just until blended.
■ Blend in melted chocolate; pour over crust.
■ Bake 55 to 60 minutes or until center is almost set. Run knife or metal spatula around rim of pan to loosen cake; cool before removing rim of pan. Refrigerate 4 hours or overnight. Garnish with chocolate curls and powdered sugar.   *12 servings*

Macadamia Nut: Stir 1 (3½ oz.) jar macadamia nuts, chopped (about ¾ cup) into batter.

Philly 3-Step™
Luscious Lemon Cheesecake

Super for spring or summer entertaining!

Prep time: *10 min.* Cooking time: *40 min.*

2	(8 oz.) pkgs. PHILADELPHIA BRAND Cream Cheese, softened
½	cup sugar
1	tablespoon fresh lemon juice
½	teaspoon grated lemon peel
½	teaspoon vanilla
2	eggs
1	KEEBLER READY CRUST™ Graham Cracker Pie Crust (6 oz. *or* 9 inch)

1. MIX cream cheese, sugar, juice, peel and vanilla at medium speed with electric mixer until well blended. Add eggs; mix until blended.

2. POUR into crust.

3. BAKE at 350°F, 40 minutes or until center is almost set. Cool. Refrigerate 3 hours or overnight. Garnish with COOL WHIP Whipped Topping and lemon slices.

8 servings

Philly 3-Step™
Fruit Topped Cheesecake

A jewel of a cheesecake.

Prep time: *10 min.* Cooking time: *40 min.*

2   (8 oz.) pkgs. PHILADELPHIA BRAND Cream Cheese, softened

½   cup sugar

½   teaspoon vanilla

2   eggs

1   KEEBLER READY CRUST™ Graham Cracker Pie Crust (6 oz. *or* 9 inch)

2   cups sliced assorted fresh fruit

2   tablespoons strawberry *or* apple jelly, heated (optional)

1. MIX cream cheese, sugar and vanilla at medium speed with electric mixer until well blended. Add eggs; mix until blended.

2. POUR into crust.

3. BAKE at 350°F, 40 minutes or until center is almost set. Cool. Refrigerate 3 hours or overnight. Top with fruit; drizzle with jelly, if desired.   *8 servings*

Lean & Luscious: Substitute PHILADELPHIA BRAND Neufchatel Cheese, ⅓ Less Fat Than Cream Cheese *or* PHILADELPHIA BRAND FREE Fat Free Cream Cheese for cream cheese.

Philly 3-Step™
Raspberry Swirl Cheesecake

The flavor of raspberries and cream are captured here.

Prep time: *10 min.* Cooking time: *40 min.*

2	(8 oz.) pkgs. PHILADELPHIA BRAND Cream Cheese, softened
½	cup sugar
½	teaspoon vanilla
2	eggs
1	KEEBLER READY CRUST™ Graham Cracker Pie Crust (6 oz. *or* 9 inch)
3	tablespoons red raspberries preserves

1. MIX cream cheese, sugar and vanilla at medium speed with electric mixer until well blended. Add eggs; mix until blended.

2. POUR into crust. Dot top of cheesecake with preserves. Cut through batter with knife several times for marble effect.

3. BAKE at 350°F, 40 minutes or until center is almost set. Cool. Refrigerate 3 hours or overnight. Garnish with COOL WHIP Whipped Topping and raspberries.

8 servings

Peaches and Cream: Substitute ¼ cup peach preserves for red raspberry preserves.

Philly 3-Step™
Blueberry Cheesecake

One of summer's simple pleasures.

Prep time: *10 min.* Cooking time: *40 min.*

2   (8 oz.) pkgs. PHILADELPHIA BRAND Cream Cheese, softened
½   cup sugar
½   teaspoon vanilla
2   eggs
1   cup blueberries, divided
1   KEEBLER READY CRUST™ Graham Cracker Pie Crust (6 oz. *or* 9 inch)

1. MIX cream cheese, sugar and vanilla at medium speed with electric mixer until well blended. Add eggs; mix until blended. Stir in ½ cup of the blueberries.

2. POUR into crust. Sprinkle with remaining ½ cup blueberries.

3. BAKE at 350°F, 40 minutes or until center is almost set. Cool. Refrigerate 3 hours or overnight. Garnish with COOL WHIP Whipped Topping and blueberries.

8 servings

Philly 3-Step™
Key Lime Cheesecake

Top off your next Mexican meal with this one!

Prep time: *10 min.* Cooking time: *40 min.*

2	(8 oz.) pkgs. PHILADELPHIA BRAND Cream Cheese, softened
½	cup sugar
2	tablespoons fresh lime juice
1	teaspoon grated lime peel
½	teaspoon vanilla
2	eggs
1	KEEBLER READY CRUST™ Graham Cracker Pie Crust (6 oz. *or* 9 inch)

1. MIX cream cheese, sugar, juice, peel and vanilla at medium speed with electric mixer until well blended. Add eggs; mix until blended.

2. POUR into crust.

3. BAKE at 350°F, 40 minutes or until center is almost set. Cool. Refrigerate 3 hours or overnight. Garnish with lime slices.

8 servings

Philly 3-Step™ Cranberry Cheesecake

Great for Thanksgiving or Christmas!

Prep time: _10 min._ Cooking time: _40 min._

2   (8 oz.) pkgs. PHILADELPHIA BRAND Cream
      Cheese, softened
½   cup sugar
½   teaspoon grated orange peel
½   teaspoon vanilla
2   eggs
¾   cup chopped cranberries divided
1   KEEBLER READY CRUST™ Graham Cracker
      Pie Crust (6 oz. _or_ 9 inch)

1. MIX cream cheese, sugar, peel and vanilla at medium speed with electric mixer until well blended. Add eggs; mix until blended. Stir in ½ cup of the cranberries.

2. POUR into crust. Sprinkle with remaining ¼ cup cranberries.

3. BAKE at 350°F, 40 minutes or until center is almost set. Cool. Refrigerate 3 hours or overnight. Garnish with cranberries, mint leaves and orange peel.   _8 servings_

Citrus Fruit Cheesecake

A subtle hint of lemon and orange brighten this classic cheesecake.

Prep time: *20 min.* Cooking time: *50 min.*

CRUST

1   cup graham cracker crumbs
⅓   cup firmly packed brown sugar
¼   cup (½ stick) PARKAY Spread Sticks, melted

FILLING

4   (8 oz.) pkgs. PHILADELPHIA BRAND Cream Cheese, softened
1   cup granulated sugar
1   teaspoon vanilla
4   eggs
1   tablespoon fresh lemon juice
1   teaspoon grated orange peel
    Sliced assorted fresh fruit

- Heat oven to 325°F.

CRUST

- Mix crumbs, brown sugar and PARKAY spread; press onto bottom of 9-inch springform pan. Bake 10 minutes.

FILLING

- Beat cream cheese, granulated sugar and vanilla at medium speed with electric mixer until well blended. Add eggs, 1 at a time, mixing at low speed after each addition, just until blended. Blend in juice and peel; pour over crust.
- Bake 45 to 50 minutes or until center is almost set. Run knife or metal spatula around rim of pan to loosen cake; cool before removing rim of pan. Refrigerate 4 hours or overnight.
- Top with fruit. Garnish with lime peel.

12 servings

Heavenly Cheesecake

This divine creation will delight your family and friends.

Prep time: *15 min.* Cooking time: *50 min.*

1/2   cup graham cracker crumbs
4   (8 oz.) pkgs. PHILADELPHIA BRAND
      Neufchatel Cheese, 1/3 Less Fat Than
      Cream Cheese *or* PHILADELPHIA BRAND FREE
      Fat Free Cream Cheese, softened
1   cup sugar
1/4   teaspoon almond extract *or* 1 teaspoon vanilla
2   eggs
3   egg whites

- Heat oven to 325°F.
- Lightly grease bottom of 9-inch springform pan. Sprinkle with crumbs.
- Beat Neufchatel cheese, sugar and extract at medium speed with electric mixer until well blended. Add eggs and egg whites, 1 at a time, mixing at low speed after each addition, just until blended. Pour into pan.
- Bake 45 to 50 minutes or until center is almost set. Run knife or metal spatula around rim of pan to loosen cake; cool before removing rim of pan. Refrigerate 4 hours or overnight.
- Garnish with raspberries, strawberries or blueberries and mint leaves.   *12 servings*

Philly 3-Step™

Pralines and Cream Cheesecake

A caramel-swirled, toffee-filled cheesecake.

Prep time: *10 min.* Cooking time: *40 min.*

2	(8 oz.) pkgs. PHILADELPHIA BRAND Cream Cheese, softened
½	cup sugar
½	teaspoon vanilla
2	eggs
½	cup almond brickle chips
1	KEEBLER READY CRUST™ Graham Cracker Pie Crust (6 oz. *or* 9 inch)
3	tablespoons caramel ice cream topping

1. MIX cream cheese, sugar and vanilla at medium speed with electric mixer until well blended. Add eggs; mix until blended. Blend in almond brickle chips.

2. POUR into crust. Dot top of cheesecake batter with topping. Cut through batter with knife several times for marble effect.

3. BAKE at 350°F, 40 minutes or until center is almost set. Cool. Refrigerate 3 hours or overnight.   *8 servings*

Philly 3-Step™
Caramel Apple Cheesecake

Serve this creation at your fall gatherings.

Prep time: *10 min.* Cooking time: *40 min.*

2   (8 oz.) pkgs. PHILADELPHIA BRAND Cream
     Cheese, softened
½   cup sugar
½   teaspoon vanilla
2   eggs
⅓   cup frozen apple juice concentrate, thawed
1   KEEBLER READY CRUST™ Graham Cracker
     Pie Crust (6 oz. *or* 9 inch)
¼   cup caramel ice cream topping
¼   cup chopped peanuts

1. MIX cream cheese, sugar and vanilla at
medium speed with electric mixer until
well blended. Add eggs; mix until
blended. Blend in juice concentrate.

2. POUR
into crust.

3. BAKE at 350°F, 40 minutes or until
center is almost set. Cool. Refrigerate 3
hours or overnight. Drizzle with topping
and sprinkle with peanuts before serving.
Garnish with apple slices.   *8 servings*

Philly 3-Step™ Rocky Road Cheesecake

Marshmallows, chocolate chips and peanuts bake into this chocolate cheesecake.

Prep time: *10 min.* Cooking time: *40 min.*

2	(8 oz.) pkgs. PHILADELPHIA BRAND Cream Cheese, softened
½	cup sugar
½	teaspoon vanilla
2	eggs
4	squares BAKER'S Semi-Sweet Chocolate, melted, slightly cooled
1	KEEBLER READY CRUST™ Graham Cracker Pie Crust (6 oz. *or* 9 inch)
½	cup miniature marshmallows
¼	cup BAKER'S Semi-Sweet Real Chocolate Chips
¼	cup chopped peanuts

1. MIX cream cheese, sugar and vanilla at medium speed with electric mixer until well blended. Add eggs; mix until blended. Blend in melted chocolate.

2. POUR into crust. Sprinkle with marshmallows, chips and peanuts.

3. BAKE at 350°F, 40 minutes or until center is almost set. Cool. Refrigerate 3 hours or overnight. Garnish with multicolored sprinkles. *8 servings*

Philly 3-Step™
Honey Crunch Cheesecake

Crunchy granola and almonds sweetened with honey make this cheesecake great!

Prep time: *10 min.* Cooking time: *40 min.*

2	(8 oz.) pkgs. PHILADELPHIA BRAND Cream Cheese, softened
⅓	cup honey
½	teaspoon vanilla
2	eggs
1	KEEBLER READY CRUST™ Graham Cracker Pie Crust (6 oz. *or* 9 inch)
½	cup granola cereal
¼	cup chopped almonds

1. MIX cream cheese, honey and vanilla at medium speed with electric mixer until well blended. Add eggs; mix until blended.

2. POUR into crust. Sprinkle with granola cereal and almonds.

3. BAKE at 350°F, 40 minutes or until center is almost set. Cool. Refrigerate 3 hours or overnight. Drizzle with honey, if desired.   *8 servings*

Philly 3-Step™
Midwest Cheesecake

A rich vanilla cheesecake topped with strawberries.

Prep time: *10 min.* Cooking time: *40 min.*

2	(8 oz.) pkgs. PHILADELPHIA BRAND Cream Cheese, softened
½	cup sugar
½	teaspoon vanilla
2	eggs
1	KEEBLER READY CRUST™ Graham Cracker Pie Crust (6 oz. *or* 9 inch)
½	cup sour cream
3	cups whole strawberries, stems removed
2	tablespoons strawberry jelly, heated

1. MIX cream cheese, sugar and vanilla at medium speed with electric mixer until well blended. Add eggs; mix until blended.

2. POUR into crust.

3. BAKE at 350°F, 40 minutes or until center is almost set. Cool. Refrigerate 3 hours or overnight. Spread sour cream over cheesecake. Top with strawberries, stem-side down. Drizzle with jelly.

8 servings

Philly 3-Step™ Crème Brûlée Cheesecake

A classic European custard inspired this exquisite cheesecake.

Prep time: *10 min.* Cooking time: *40 min.*

2   (8 oz.) pkgs. PHILADELPHIA BRAND Cream Cheese, softened
½   cup granulated sugar
1   teaspoon vanilla
2   eggs
1   egg yolk
1   KEEBLER READY CRUST™ Graham Cracker Pie Crust (6 oz. *or* 9 inch)
½   cup packed brown sugar
1   teaspoon water

1. MIX cream cheese, granulated sugar and vanilla at medium speed with electric mixer until well blended. Add eggs and egg yolk; mix until blended.

2. POUR into crust.

3. BAKE at 350°F, 40 minutes or until center is almost set. Cool. Refrigerate 3 hours or overnight. Just before serving, heat broiler. Mix brown sugar and water; spread over cheesecake. Place on cookie sheet. Broil 4 to 6 inches from heat 1 to 1½ minutes or until topping is bubbly.

8 servings

New York Cheesecake

One of the classics!

Prep time: *25 min.* Cooking time: *1 hour 10 min.*

CRUST
1	cup graham cracker crumbs
3	tablespoons sugar
3	tablespoons PARKAY Spread Sticks, melted

FILLING
4	(8 oz.) pkgs. PHILADELPHIA BRAND Cream Cheese, softened
1	cup sugar
3	tablespoons flour
1	tablespoon vanilla
4	eggs
1	cup sour cream

TOPPING (optional)
1	(21 oz.) can cherry pie filling *or* 3 cups whole strawberries, stems removed

■ Heat oven to 325°F.

CRUST

■ Mix crumbs, sugar and PARKAY spread;
press onto bottom of 9-inch springform pan.
Bake 10 minutes.

FILLING

■ Beat cream cheese, sugar, flour and vanilla at
medium speed with electric mixer until well
blended. Add eggs, 1 at a time, mixing at low
speed after each addition, just until blended.
■ Blend in sour cream; pour over crust.
■ Bake 1 hour and 5 minutes to 1 hour and 10
minutes or until center is almost set. Run knife
or metal spatula around rim of pan to loosen
cake; cool before removing rim of pan.
Refrigerate 4 hours or overnight.

TOPPING

■ Top with pie filling or strawberries, stem-side
down, just before serving. *12 servings*

Hollywood Cheesecake

Light and airy cheesecake with a sour cream topping.

Prep time: *25 min.* Cooking time: *55 min.*

CRUST

1	cup graham cracker crumbs
3	tablespoons sugar
3	tablespoons PARKAY Spread Sticks, melted

FILLING

2	(8 oz.) pkgs. PHILADELPHIA BRAND Cream Cheese, softened
½	cup sugar
1	tablespoon fresh lemon juice (optional)
1	teaspoon grated lemon peel (optional)
½	teaspoon vanilla
2	eggs, separated

TOPPING

1	cup sour cream
2	tablespoons sugar
1	teaspoon vanilla

■ Heat oven to 325° F.

CRUST

■ Mix crumbs, sugar and PARKAY spread; press onto bottom of 9-inch springform pan. Bake 10 minutes.

FILLING

■ Reduce oven temperature to 300°F.

■ Beat cream cheese, sugar, juice, peel and vanilla at medium speed with electric mixer until well blended. Add egg yolks, 1 at a time, mixing at low speed after each addition, just until blended. Fold in stiffly beaten egg whites; pour over crust.

■ Bake 45 minutes or until center is almost set.

TOPPING

■ Mix sour cream, sugar and vanilla. Carefully spread over cheesecake; continue baking 10 minutes. Run knife or metal spatula around rim of pan to loosen cake; cool before removing rim of pan. Refrigerate 4 hours or overnight.

■ Top with strawberry slices, raspberries and mint leaves before serving, if desired.   *12 servings*

Boston Cream Cheesecake

Boston Cream Pie transformed into a mouthwatering cheesecake.

Prep time: *25 min.* Cooking time: *55 min.*

CAKE BOTTOM
1   (9oz.) pkg. yellow cake mix (one layer size)

FILLING
2   (8 oz.) pkgs. PHILADELPHIA BRAND Cream
      Cheese, softened
1/2 cup granulated sugar
1   teaspoon vanilla
2   eggs
1/3 cup sour cream

TOPPING
2   squares BAKER'S Unsweetened Chocolate
3   tablespoons PARKAY Spread Sticks
2   tablespoons boiling water
1   cup powdered sugar
1   teaspoon vanilla

■ Heat oven to 350° F.

CAKE BOTTOM
■ Grease bottom of 9-inch springform pan. Prepare cake mix as directed on package; pour batter evenly into springform pan. Bake 20 minutes.

FILLING
■ Beat cream cheese, sugar and vanilla at medium speed with electric mixer until well blended. Add eggs, 1 at a time, mixing at low speed after each addition, just until blended. Blend in sour cream; pour over cake layer.
■ Bake 35 minutes or until center is almost set. Run knife or metal spatula around rim of pan to loosen cake; cool before removing rim of pan.

TOPPING
■ Melt chocolate and PARKAY spread over low heat, stirring until smooth. Remove from heat. Add water and remaining ingredients; mix well. Spread over cooled cheesecake. Refrigerate 4 hours or overnight.   *12 servings*

Philly 3-Step™
Pumpkin Cheesecake

A festive finale for your Thanksgiving meal.

Prep time: *10 min.* Cooking time: *40 min.*

2   (8 oz.) pkgs. PHILADELPHIA BRAND Cream
    Cheese, softened
½   cup canned pumpkin
½   cup sugar
½   teaspoon vanilla
½   teaspoon ground cinnamon
    Dash *each* ground cloves and nutmeg
2   eggs
1   KEEBLER READY CRUST™ Graham Cracker
    Pie Crust (6 oz. *or* 9 inch)

1. MIX cream cheese, pumpkin, sugar, vanilla and
spices at medium speed with electric mixer until
well blended. Add eggs; mix until blended.

2. POUR
into crust.

3. BAKE at 350°F, 40 minutes or until center is
almost set. Cool. Refrigerate 3 hours or overnight.
Garnish with COOL WHIP Whipped Topping and
chocolate dipped pecans.   *8 servings*

Pumpkin Chocolate Chip: Stir ½ cup mini semi-
sweet chocolate chips into batter. Sprinkle with
additional ¼ cup chips before baking.

Pumpkin Praline Pecan: Substitiute ½ cup
packed brown sugar for granulated sugar.
Sprinkle with 1 cup chopped pecans before
baking. Drizzle chilled baked cheesecake with 2
tablespoons maple flavored syrup.

Philly 3-Step™
Coconut Cheesecake

For a festive Easter dessert, garnish with jelly beans and serve in a basket.

Prep time: *10 min.* Cooking time: *40 min.*

2   (8 oz.) pkgs. PHILADELPHIA BRAND Cream Cheese, softened
½   cup cream of coconut
½   cup sugar
½   teaspoon vanilla
2   eggs
1   KEEBLER READY CRUST™ Graham Cracker Pie Crust (6 oz. *or* 9 inch)
1   cup COOL WHIP Whipped Topping, thawed
½   cup BAKER'S ANGEL FLAKE Coconut, toasted

1. MIX cream cheese, cream of coconut, sugar and vanilla at medium speed with electric mixer until well blended. Add eggs; mix until blended.

2. POUR into crust.

3. BAKE at 350°F, 40 minutes or until center is almost set. Cool. Refrigerate 3 hours or overnight. Top with whipped topping and toasted coconut before serving.   *8 servings*

Philly 3-Step™

Rainbow Candy Cheesecake

Bake this for birthday parties!

Prep time: *10 min.* Cooking time: *40 min.*

2   (8 oz.) pkgs. PHILADELPHIA BRAND Cream Cheese, softened
½   cup sugar
½   teaspoon vanilla
2   eggs
1   KEEBLER READY CRUST™ Graham Cracker Pie Crust (6 oz. *or* 9 inch)
½   cup COOL WHIP Whipped Topping, thawed
½   cup multicolored milk chocolate candies

1. MIX cream cheese, sugar and vanilla at medium speed with electric mixer until well blended. Add eggs; mix until blended.

2. POUR into crust.

3. BAKE at 350°F, 40 minutes or until center is almost set. Cool. Refrigerate 3 hours or overnight. Spread with whipped topping; sprinkle with candies.   *8 servings*

Philly 3-Step™
Peppermint Stick Cheesecake

Christmas calls for this pretty pink confection.

Prep time: *10 min.* Cooking time: *40 min.*

2   (8 oz.) pkgs. PHILADELPHIA BRAND Cream Cheese, softened
½   cup sugar
½   teaspoon vanilla
2   eggs
¾   cup finely crushed peppermint candy, divided
1   KEEBLER READY CRUST™ Graham Cracker Pie Crust (6 oz. *or* 9 inch)

1. MIX cream cheese, sugar and vanilla at medium speed with electric mixer until well blended. Add eggs; mix until blended. Stir in ½ cup of the peppermint candy.

2. POUR into crust. Sprinkle with remaining ¼ cup peppermint candy.

3. BAKE at 350°F, 40 minutes or until center is almost set. Cool. Refrigerate 3 hours or overnight. Garnish with COOL WHIP Whipped Topping and crushed peppermint candy.   *8 servings*

Confetti Sprinkles: Omit peppermint candy. Stir 3 tablespoons multicolored sprinkles into batter. Top with additional 2 tablespoons sprinkles before baking.

Philly 3-Step™ Chocolate Chip Cookie Dough Cheesecake

Created for cookie dough lovers!

Prep time: *10 min.* Cooking time: *40 min.*

2	(8 oz.) pkgs. PHILADELPHIA BRAND Cream Cheese, softened
½	cup sugar
½	teaspoon vanilla
2	eggs
¾	cup prepared chocolate chip cookie dough, divided
1	KEEBLER READY CRUST™ Graham Cracker Pie Crust (6 oz. *or* 9 inch)

1. MIX cream cheese, sugar and vanilla at medium speed with electric mixer until well blended. Add eggs; mix until blended. Drop ½ cup of the cookie dough by level teaspoonfuls into batter; fold gently.

2. POUR into crust. Dot with level teaspoonfuls of remaining ¼ cup cookie dough.

3. BAKE at 350°F, 40 minutes or until center is almost set. Cool. Refrigerate 3 hours or overnight. *8 servings*

Cookies and Cream: Omit cookie dough. Substitute chocolate flavored pie crust for graham cracker pie crust. Stir ½ cup chopped chocolate sandwich cookies into batter. Sprinkle with additional ¼ cup chopped chocolate sandwich cookies before baking.

Philly 3-Step™ Mini Cheesecakes

Create your own taste sensations!

Prep time: *10 min.* Cooking time: *20 min.*

2 (8 oz.) pkgs. PHILADELPHIA BRAND Cream
   Cheese, softened
½ cup sugar
½ teaspoon vanilla
2 eggs
2 (4 oz.) pkgs. KEEBLER READY CRUST™ Single Serve
   Graham Cracker Pie Crusts (12 crusts)
   COOL WHIP Whipped Topping, thawed
   Assorted tiny candies

1. MIX cream cheese, sugar and vanilla at medium speed with electric mixer until well blended. Add eggs; mix until blended.

2. POUR into crusts placed on cookie sheet.

3. BAKE at 350°F, 20 minutes or until centers are almost set. Cool. Refrigerate 2 hours or overnight. Top with whipped topping and sprinkle with multicolored milk chocolate candies, candy corn, gummy bears or other tiny candies just before serving.   *12 servings*

Philly 3-Step™
Toffee Crunch Cheesecake

Toffee-topped cheesecake perfect for holidays or anytime.

Prep time: *10 min.* Cooking time: *40 min.*

2	(8 oz.) pkgs. PHILADELPHIA BRAND Cream Cheese, softened
½	cup sugar
½	teaspoon vanilla
2	eggs
1	KEEBLER READY CRUST™ Graham Cracker Pie Crust (6 oz. *or* 9 inch)
4	(1.4 oz.) bars chocolate covered English toffee, chopped (1 cup)

1. MIX cream cheese, sugar and vanilla at medium speed with electric mixer until well blended. Add eggs; mix until blended.

2. POUR into crust. Sprinkle with toffee.

3. BAKE at 350°F, 40 minutes or until center is almost set. Cool. Refrigerate 3 hours or overnight. *8 servings*

Peanut Butter Caramel Nut: Omit toffee. Beat ⅓ cup peanut butter in with cream cheese. Sprinkle with 1 cup chopped milk chocolate with nuts and caramel candy bars (three 2.07 oz. bars) before baking.

Cookies and Cream Cheesecake

A chocolate cookie-studded cheesecake.

Prep time: *25 min.* Cooking time: *1 hour 5 min.*

CRUST
1   cup finely crushed chocolate sandwich
    cookies
1   tablespoon PARKAY Spread Sticks, melted

FILLING
3   (8 oz.) pkgs. PHILADELPHIA BRAND Cream
    Cheese, softened
1   cup sugar
2   tablespoons flour
1   teaspoon vanilla
3   eggs
1   cup coarsely chopped chocolate sandwich
    cookies

■ Heat oven to 325°F.

CRUST
■ Mix crumbs, and PARKAY spread; press onto
  bottom of 9-inch springform pan. Bake 10 minutes.

FILLING
■ Beat cream cheese, sugar, flour and vanilla at
  medium speed with electric mixer until well
  blended. Add eggs, 1 at a time, mixing at low
  speed after each addition, just until blended.
■ Fold in chopped cookies; pour over crust.
■ Bake 1 hour and 5 minutes or until center is
  almost set. Run knife or metal spatula around
  rim of pan to loosen cake; cool before removing
  rim of pan. Refrigerate 4 hours or overnight.
  Garnish with COOL WHIP Whipped Topping,
  chocolate sandwich cookies, cut in half, and
  mint leaves.   *12 servings*

Philly 3-Step™
Crème de Menthe Cheesecake

Fun for St. Patrick's Day!

Prep time: *10 min.* Cooking time: *40 min.*

2   (8 oz.) pkgs. PHILADELPHIA BRAND Cream Cheese, softened
½   cup sugar
½   teaspoon vanilla
2   eggs
4   teaspoons green crème de menthe
1   KEEBLER READY CRUST™ Chocolate Flavored Pie Crust (6 oz. *or* 9 inch)

1.
MIX cream cheese, sugar and vanilla at medium speed with electric mixer until well blended. Add eggs; mix until blended. Blend in crème de menthe.

2.
POUR into crust.

3.
BAKE at 350°F, 40 minutes or until center is almost set. Cool. Refrigerate 3 hours or overnight. Garnish with chocolate leaves and twigs.   *8 servings*

Mint Bon Bon: Substitute ¼ teaspoon peppermint extract and a few drops green food coloring for crème de menthe. Stir ½ cup mini semi-sweet chocolate chips into batter. Sprinkle with additional ¼ cup chips before baking.

Philly 3-Step™
Piña Colada Cheesecake

Try at your next barbeque.

Prep time: *10 min.* Cooking time: *40 min.*

2	(8 oz.) pkgs. PHILADELPHIA BRAND Cream Cheese, softened
½	cup sugar
½	teaspoon vanilla
2	eggs
⅓	cup piña colada frozen concentrated tropical fruit mixer, thawed
1	KEEBLER READY CRUST™ Graham Cracker Pie Crust (6 oz. *or* 9 inch)

1.
MIX cream cheese, sugar and vanilla at medium speed with electric mixer until well blended. Add eggs; mix until blended. Blend in piña colada mixer.

2.
POUR into crust.

3.
BAKE at 350°F, 40 minutes or until center is almost set. Cool. Refrigerate 3 hours or overnight. Garnish with fresh fruit. Serve with Crimson Raspberry Sauce if desired.   *8 servings*

Strawberry Daiquiri: Substitute strawberry daiquiri frozen concentrated tropical fruit mixer, thawed, for piña colada mixer.

Lime Margarita: Substitute margarita frozen concentrated tropical fruit mixer, thawed, for piña colada mixer.

Philly 3-Step™
Tirami Su Cheesecake

Our interpretation of a classic Italian treat.

Prep time: *10 min.* Cooking time: *40 min.*

2	(8 oz.) pkgs. PHILADELPHIA BRAND Cream Cheese, softened
½	cup sugar
½	teaspoon vanilla
2	eggs
2	tablespoons brandy
12	ladyfingers, split
½	cup strong black coffee
1	cup COOL WHIP Whipped Topping, thawed
1	square BAKER'S Semi-Sweet Chocolate, shaved

1. MIX cream cheese, sugar and vanilla at medium speed with electric mixer until well blended. Add eggs; mix until blended. Blend in brandy. Arrange ladyfingers on bottom and sides of 9-inch pie plate; drizzle with coffee.

2. POUR cream cheese mixture into prepared pie plate.

3. BAKE at 350°F, 40 minutes or until center is almost set. Cool. Refrigerate 3 hours or overnight. Garnish with whipped topping and shaved chocolate just before serving.   *8 servings*

Amaretto Macaroon Cheesecake

A moist chewy macaroon crust sets this almond flavored cheesecake apart from the rest.

Prep time: *25 min.* Cooking time: *1 hour*

CRUST

1   (7 oz.) pkg. BAKER'S ANGEL FLAKE Coconut, lightly toasted
½   cup finely chopped almonds, lightly toasted
1   (14 oz.) can sweetened condensed milk, divided
⅓   cup flour
¼   cup (½ stick) PARKAY Spread Sticks, melted

FILLING

4   (8 oz.) pkgs. PHILADELPHIA BRAND Cream Cheese, softened
¼   cup sugar
4   eggs
¼   cup almond-flavored liqueur

- Heat oven to 325°F.

CRUST

- Mix coconut, almonds, ½ cup of the sweetened condensed milk, flour and PARKAY spread; press onto bottom of 9-inch springform pan.

FILLING

- Beat cream cheese, sugar and remaining ¾ cup sweetened condensed milk at medium speed with electric mixer until well blended. Add eggs, 1 at a time, mixing at low speed after each addition, just until blended.
- Blend in liqueur; pour over crust.
- Bake 55 to 60 minutes or until center is almost set. Run knife or metal spatula around rim of pan to loosen cake; cool before removing rim of pan. Refrigerate 4 hours or overnight. Garnish with toasted sliced almonds and colored sugar.   *12 servings*

Cappuccino Cheesecake

A sophisticated blend of rich dark coffee and creamy cheesecake for special occasions.

Prep time: *25 min.* Cooking time: *1 hour*

CRUST
2	cups graham cracker crumbs
⅓	cup sugar
6	tablespoons PARKAY Spread Sticks, melted

FILLING
3	tablespoons coffee-flavored liqueur
1	tablespoon instant coffee
4	(8 oz.) pkgs. PHILADELPHIA BRAND Cream Cheese, softened
1	cup sugar
2	tablespoons flour
2	teaspoons vanilla
4	eggs

■ Heat oven to 325° F.

CRUST
■ Mix crumbs, sugar and PARKAY spread;
press onto bottom and 2-inches up sides of
9-inch springform pan.
Bake 10 minutes.

FILLING
■ Combine liqueur and instant coffee; stir to dissolve.
Set aside.
■ Beat cream cheese, sugar, flour and vanilla at medium
speed with electric mixer until well blended. Add eggs,
1 at a time, mixing at low speed after each addition,
just until blended.
■ Blend in coffee mixture; pour into crust.
■ Bake 55 to 60 minutes or until center is almost set.
Run knife or metal spatula around rim of pan to
loosen cake; cool before removing rim of pan.
Refrigerate 4 hours or overnight. Garnish with
chocolate dipped almonds or chocolate covered
coffee beans.   *12 servings*

Eggnog Cheesecake

Toast the holiday season with this sensational cheesecake. Cheers!

Prep time: *25 min.* Cooking time: *1 hour 15 min.*

CRUST
2   cups vanilla wafer crumbs
6   tablespoons PARKAY Spread Sticks, melted
½   teaspoon ground nutmeg

FILLING
4   (8 oz.) pkgs. PHILADELPHIA BRAND Cream Cheese, softened
1   cup sugar
3   tablespoons flour
3   tablespoons rum
1   teaspoon vanilla
2   eggs
1   cup whipping cream
4   egg yolks

- Heat oven to 325°F.

CRUST
- Mix crumbs, PARKAY spread and nutmeg; press onto bottom and 1½-inches up sides of 9-inch springform pan. Bake 10 minutes.

FILLING
- Beat cream cheese, sugar, flour, rum and vanilla at medium speed with electric mixer until well blended. Add eggs, 1 at a time, mixing at low speed after each addition, just until blended.
- Blend in cream and egg yolks; pour into crust.
- Bake 1 hour and 10 minutes to 1 hour and 15 minutes or until center is almost set. Run knife or metal spatula around rim of pan to loosen cake; cool before removing rim of pan. Refrigerate 4 hours or overnight. Garnish with COOL WHIP Whipped Topping and ground nutmeg.   *12 servings*

PHILLY 3-STEP™ Cheesecakes

Springform Pan Cheesecakes

Special Occasion Flavor Suggestions

New Year's PHILLY 3-STEP™ Tirami Su Cheesecake
Chocolate Truffle Cheesecake

Valentine's Day PHILLY 3-STEP™ Midwest Cheesecake
Chocolate Raspberry Cheesecake

St. Patrick's Day PHILLY 3-STEP™ Crème de Menthe Cheesecake

Easter PHILLY 3-STEP™ Coconut Cheesecake
PHILLY 3-STEP™ Luscious Lemon Cheesecake

Mother's Day PHILLY 3-STEP™ Fruit Topped Cheesecake
White Chocolate Cheesecake

Memorial Day PHILLY 3-STEP™ Pralines and Cream
Cheesecake
PHILLY 3-STEP™ Rocky Road Cheesecake

Father's Day PHILLY 3-STEP™ Toffee Crunch Cheesecake
New York Cheesecake

Graduation Day PHILLY 3-STEP™ Chocolate Chip Cheesecake
Brownie Bottom Cheesecake

Fourth of July PHILLY 3-STEP™ Blueberry Cheesecake

Labor Day PHILLY 3-STEP™ Piña Colada Cheesecake

Rosh Hashanah PHILLY 3-STEP™ Honey Crunch Cheesecake

Halloween PHILLY 3-STEP™ Caramel Apple Cheesecake
PHILLY 3-STEP™ Mini Cheesecakes

Thanksgiving PHILLY 3-STEP™ Pumpkin Cheesecake
PHILLY 3-STEP™ Cranberry Cheesecake

Hanukkah PHILLY 3-STEP™ White Chocolate
Almond Cheesecake

Christmas PHILLY 3-STEP™ Peppermint Stick Cheesecake
Eggnog Cheesecake